The Next Level Forgiver

Release the Pain

Embrace the Peace

Work Booklet

C.L. Holley

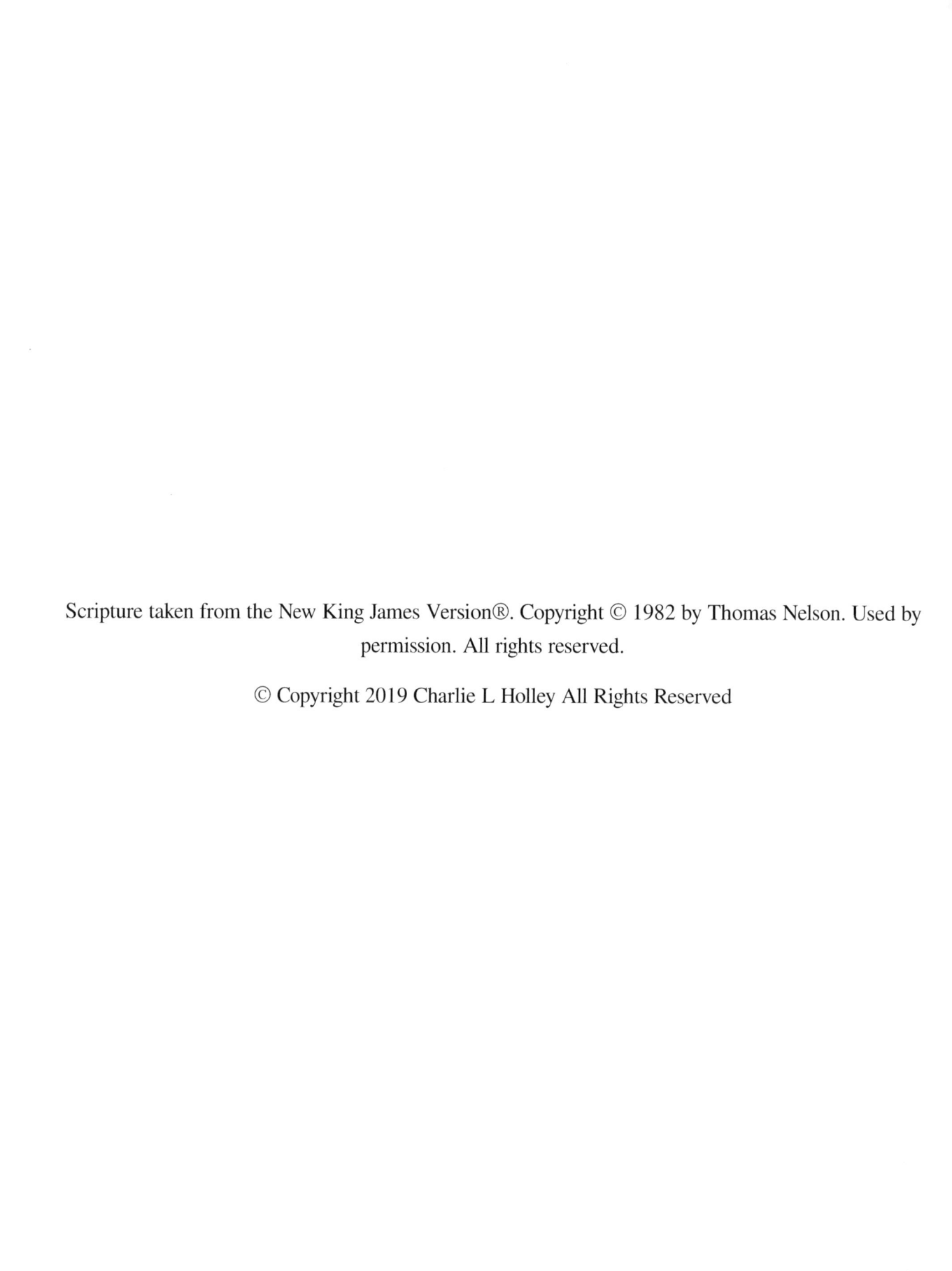

Scripture taken from the New King James Version®. Copyright © 1982 by Thomas Nelson. Used by permission. All rights reserved.

© Copyright 2019 Charlie L Holley All Rights Reserved

TABLE OF CONTENTS

Introduction	7
Exercise 1: Have You Acknowledged the Hurt?	9
Exercise 2: Have You Covered or Conquered?	21
Exercise 3: Level Zero. Are You Here?	33
Exercise 4: Level One. Are You Here?	45
Exercise 5: Level Two. Are You Here?	57
Exercise 6: Level Three. Am I Here?	69
Exercise 7: Have You Adopted Postures and Practiced Principles?	81
Exercise 8: Have You Forgiven Persecution?	93
Exercise 9: Have You Forgiven Yourself?	105
Exercise 10: Have You Recognized the Enemies of Forgiveness?	117
Exercise 11: Have You Walked through the Process?	129
Exercise 12: Do You Realize It's Not About You?	141
Forgiveness Journal	154
Other Books by C.L. Holley	165

INTRODUCTION

What can happen in twelve days? Much if you accept this twelve-day challenge to read the book and do the exercises in this work booklet. I believe invisible walls of heavy sadness and depression will crumble and peace will overflow your life in ways you never knew possible.

I also believe people will see a different person in you—happier, brighter, and filled with the love of Christ.

That's what perfect forgiveness does. It changes you from the inside out. It releases you from the guilt, pain, and anger and fills your being with the peace and joy that people tend to notice. Some may not speak of it. Others may admire from afar. But there will be no doubt about your brilliant transformation.

I don't know you. I don't know your story, pain, or challenge. But I am familiar with the power of forgiveness. When done properly, in perfection, it can usher in freedom from the life-robbing emotions of hatred and anger.

Yet despite unforgiveness, life for millions of people around the world goes on. Perhaps you are one of those who tries to avoid thinking about it. Perhaps you have convinced yourself of your own guilt or imperfection that may have contributed to the abuse, abandonment, or assault.

Maybe you've tried to forgive and let go many times. Still, for some reason, the haunting thoughts of the past remain powerful, and you can't bring yourself to truly let go of the hurt. So you settle and believe avoiding the topic is the best relief you will ever get.

It's not too late for healing. The good days are not gone. And if you accept this challenge, a great breath of peace awaits you. It won't be easy. In fact, it will be difficult. But I believe the end reward of freedom is worth the long journey to forgiveness. .

This work booklet contains twelve exercises, some with deep questions about hurtful moments in your life. I ask you to do those you are ready to face. Work your way, chapter-by-chapter and exercise-by-exercise, out of pain and into peace.

This work booklet is the companion for the book, *The Next Level Forgiver*. For best results, please use this booklet with the book itself. I highly recommend reading a chapter in the book, then do an exercise in the work booklet—continuing that pattern until all twelve exercises are completed.

Please be as honest and open as possible. You can write as much or as little as you feel necessary. If you are writing about a sensitive topic and do not want to reveal true identities, feel free to change names (e.g. John Doe), use abbreviations, or employ any other means to conceal a person's real identity.

Below is a suggested schedule. It is not set in stone but merely a guideline. Feel free to modify it or develop one that will accommodate your personal or group study time.

    Day 1: Book Introduction + work booklet Exercise 1
    Day 2: Book Chapter 1 + work booklet Exercise 2
    Day 3: Book Chapter 2 + work booklet Exercise 3
    Day 4: Book Chapter 3 + work booklet Exercise 4
    Day 5: Book Chapter 4 + work booklet Exercise 5
    Day 6: Book Chapter 5 + work booklet Exercise 6
    Day 7: Book Chapter 6 + work booklet Exercise 7
    Day 8: Book Chapter 7 + work booklet Exercise 8
    Day 9: Book Chapter 8 + work booklet Exercise 9
    Day 10: Book Chapter 9 + work booklet Exercise 10
    Day 11: Book Chapter 10 + work booklet Exercise 11
    Day 12: Book Chapter 11 + work booklet Exercise 12

EXERCISE

1

HAVE YOU ACKNOWLEDGED THE HURT?

In the book, I share a true story of my older brother who finally confided in me about a troubling incident in his early childhood. He had concealed that hurtful event for over fifty years. I also shared his past and concluded with my beliefs about the role unresolved issues played in his life. I believe he covered the hurt, not conquered it.

What about you? Have you faced the giants of hurt in your life and worked your way through the painful emotions? Have you adopted the misguided practice of moving on with your life without confronting unpleasant situations?

The purpose of this exercise is to bring those unwelcomed memories to the forefront of your mind, as painful as they might be. Through much confession and expression, you can master the haunting occurrences that stole your joy.

Book quotes:

> "Every negative event in your life should be confronted, but not everything should become public."

> "You cannot conquer what you refuse to confront."

> "But it takes more energy to conceal your emotions and pain than it does to freely express them."

> "Some of us are introverts who shy away from human interaction—making sharing our hurt more difficult. Still others are extroverts who welcome interaction and have no problems sharing hurtful things."

Exercise 1 Instructions

If possible, please read the Introduction in the book *The Next Level Forgiver* and follow the instructions below.

Write as little or as much as you want about the painful events in your life.

You can use one word, one sentence, or one paragraph. But please write something to indicate you acknowledge the incident occurred.

Include all events that had or may still have a significant impact on you no matter how long it has been.

Please answer any questions as well as you can.

If you prefer not to reveal real names or situations, feel free to use general names (e.g. John, Jane, he, she), initials, or even code names or words that only you will recognize.

To-Dos (Please choose at least one):

Confide in someone you trust.

Start a journal. (There is space at the end of this work booklet.)

Confess it in prayer to God—tell Him all your feelings.

Exercise 1 Questions

Incident: 1

When did this occur?
[ ] Recently   [ ] 1-5 yrs ago   [ ] 5-10yrs ago   [ ] over 10yrs ago

Who was involved? (Optional—you don't have to answer this.):

What happened?

How did it affect you? What feelings and/or thoughts did you experience?

Do you still struggle with those feelings and/or thoughts?

Do you think you have forgiven?
[ ] Yes,   [ ] No, I have not   [ ] I try but struggle   [ ] I'm not sure

Why do you think you have or have not forgiven? How can you tell?

Exercise 1 Questions

Incident: 2

When did this occur?
[ ] Recently   [ ] 1-5 yrs ago   [ ] 5-10yrs ago   [ ] over 10yrs ago

Who was involved? (Optional—you don't have to answer this.):

What happened?

How did it affect you? What feelings and/or thoughts did you experience?

Do you still struggle with those feelings and/or thoughts?

Do you think you have forgiven?
[ ] Yes,   [ ] No, I have not   [ ] I try but struggle   [ ] I'm not sure

Why do you think you have or have not forgiven? How can you tell?

Exercise 1 Questions

Incident: 3

When did this occur?
[ ] Recently   [ ] 1-5 yrs ago   [ ] 5-10yrs ago   [ ] over 10yrs ago

Who was involved? (Optional—you don't have to answer this.):

What happened?

How did it affect you? What feelings and/or thoughts did you experience?

Do you still struggle with those feelings and/or thoughts?

Do you think you have forgiven?
[ ] Yes,   [ ] No, I have not   [ ] I try but struggle   [ ] I'm not sure

Why do you think you have or have not forgiven? How can you tell?

THE NEXT LEVEL FORGIVER WORK BOOKLET

Exercise 1 Questions

Incident: 4

When did this occur?
[ ] Recently   [ ] 1-5 yrs ago   [ ] 5-10yrs ago   [ ] over 10yrs ago

Who was involved? (Optional—you don't have to answer this.):

What happened?

How did it affect you? What feelings and/or thoughts did you experience?

Do you still struggle with those feelings and/or thoughts?

Do you think you have forgiven?
[ ] Yes,   [ ] No, I have not   [ ] I try but struggle   [ ] I'm not sure

Why do you think you have or have not forgiven? How can you tell?

Exercise 1 Questions

Incident: 5

When did this occur?
[ ] Recently   [ ] 1-5 yrs ago   [ ] 5-10yrs ago   [ ] over 10yrs ago

Who was involved? (Optional—you don't have to answer this.):

What happened?

How did it affect you? What feelings and/or thoughts did you experience?

Do you still struggle with those feelings and/or thoughts?

Do you think you have forgiven?
[ ] Yes,   [ ] No, I have not   [ ] I try but struggle   [ ] I'm not sure

Why do you think you have or have not forgiven? How can you tell?

Exercise 1 Questions

Incident: 6

When did this occur?
[ ] Recently   [ ] 1-5 yrs ago   [ ] 5-10yrs ago   [ ] over 10yrs ago

Who was involved? (Optional—you don't have to answer this.):

What happened?

How did it affect you? What feelings and/or thoughts did you experience?

Do you still struggle with those feelings and/or thoughts?

Do you think you have forgiven?
[ ] Yes,   [ ] No, I have not   [ ] I try but struggle   [ ] I'm not sure

Why do you think you have or have not forgiven? How can you tell?

Exercise 1 Questions

Incident: 7

When did this occur?

[ ] Recently   [ ] 1-5 yrs ago   [ ] 5-10yrs ago   [ ] over 10yrs ago

Who was involved? (Optional—you don't have to answer this.):

What happened?

How did it affect you? What feelings and/or thoughts did you experience?

Do you still struggle with those feelings and/or thoughts?

Do you think you have forgiven?

[ ] Yes,   [ ] No, I have not   [ ] I try but struggle   [ ] I'm not sure

Why do you think you have or have not forgiven? How can you tell?

THE NEXT LEVEL FORGIVER WORK BOOKLET

Exercise 1 Questions

Incident: 8

When did this occur?
[ ] Recently   [ ] 1-5 yrs ago   [ ] 5-10yrs ago   [ ] over 10yrs ago

Who was involved? (Optional—you don't have to answer this.):

What happened?

How did it affect you? What feelings and/or thoughts did you experience?

Do you still struggle with those feelings and/or thoughts?

Do you think you have forgiven?
[ ] Yes,   [ ] No, I have not   [ ] I try but struggle   [ ] I'm not sure

Why do you think you have or have not forgiven? How can you tell?

Exercise 1 Questions

Incident: 9

When did this occur?
[ ] Recently   [ ] 1-5 yrs ago   [ ] 5-10yrs ago   [ ] over 10yrs ago

Who was involved? (Optional—you don't have to answer this.):

What happened?

How did it affect you? What feelings and/or thoughts did you experience?

Do you still struggle with those feelings and/or thoughts?

Do you think you have forgiven?
[ ] Yes,   [ ] No, I have not   [ ] I try but struggle   [ ] I'm not sure

Why do you think you have or have not forgiven? How can you tell?

THE NEXT LEVEL FORGIVER WORK BOOKLET

Exercise 1 Questions

Incident: 10

When did this occur?
[ ] Recently   [ ] 1-5 yrs ago   [ ] 5-10yrs ago   [ ] over 10yrs ago

Who was involved? (Optional—you don't have to answer this.):

What happened?

How did it affect you? What feelings and/or thoughts did you experience?

Do you still struggle with those feelings and/or thoughts?

Do you think you have forgiven?
[ ] Yes,   [ ] No, I have not   [ ] I try but struggle   [ ] I'm not sure

Why do you think you have or have not forgiven? How can you tell?

Exercise

2

Have You Covered or Conquered?

Have you covered or conquered the hurtful incidents in your life? I share details in the book about differences between the two. I will summarize here.

Cover:

I refuse to talk about it or address it in any way to anyone.

The feelings have not improved. They are still as hurtful as when it occurred.

The few times I do think or talk about it, I do so in a negative manner.

It has made me bitter (untrusting or unloving toward others) instead of better.

I have no testimony regarding it, only a sad story that I am reluctant to share.

Conquer:

I talk about it when led to do so.

The feelings are not as hurtful.

When I talk about it, I do so in a constructive manner.

It has made me better (wiser, more forgiving, more patient) instead of bitter.

It has become a testimony I share to help people facing similar situations.

Book Quotes:

"Where are you concerning your tragedy? Have you overcome the crippling sense of despair from the sexual abuse, rape, or molestation? Have you conquered the anger that captured your heart when your loved one was violently and senselessly murdered? Have you dealt with the shame of the betrayal from the person you once trusted and loved with all your heart? Have the haunting questions been answered about the abandonment of those who should have loved, cared for, and protected you?"

Exercise 2 Instructions

If possible, please read chapter one in the book *The Next Level Forgiver* and follow the instructions below to the best of your ability. I recommend doing any to-dos in the exercises that apply to you.

If needed, reread the summary of conquering versus covering in this booklet to answer any questions.

For each incident you listed in exercise 1, please indicate if you have conquered or covered. If there are any incidents that have been covered, make note of them. Later in the booklet, we will determine what needs to happen to move to the next level.

To-Dos:

For every covered incident, please circle that incident number in the workbook indicating it is an area that needs work. Think about and later decide what you need to do to conquer. If necessary, make a plan as to how you will conquer. Do it one incident at a time so you will not become overwhelmed. Conquer one and then move to the next.

Exercise 2 Questions

Please check all that apply to you about the incident you identified in exercise 1.

Incident: 1

Cover

[ ] I refuse to talk about it or address it in any way to anyone—including God.

[ ] The feelings are still hurtful and thoughts and memories still vivid.

[ ] The few times I do think or talk about it, I do so in a negative manner.

[ ] It has made me bitter (untrusting or unloving toward someone) instead of better.

[ ] I have no testimony regarding it, only a sad story that I hate to share..

Conquer:

[ ] I talk about it when led to in order to help others.

[ ] The feelings are not as hurtful and thoughts and memories not as vivid.

[ ] When I talk about it, I don't demonize the person who hurt me.

[ ] It has made me better (wiser, more forgiving, more patient) instead of bitter.

[ ] It has become a testimony that I share with people in similar situations.

Have you covered or conquered this incident? Write your conclusion below:

Exercise 2 Questions

Please check all that apply to you about the incident you identified in exercise 1.

Incident: 2

Cover

[ ] I refuse to talk about it or address it in any way to anyone—including God.

[ ] The feelings are still hurtful and thoughts and memories still vivid.

[ ] The few times I do think or talk about it, I do so in a negative manner.

[ ] It has made me bitter (untrusting or unloving toward someone) instead of better.

[ ] I have no testimony regarding it, only a sad story that I hate to share..

Conquer:

[ ] I talk about it when led to in order to help others.

[ ] The feelings are not as hurtful and thoughts and memories not as vivid.

[ ] When I talk about it, I don't demonize the person who hurt me.

[ ] It has made me better (wiser, more forgiving, more patient) instead of bitter.

[ ] It has become a testimony that I share with people in similar situations.

Have you covered or conquered this incident? Write your conclusion below:

Exercise 2 Questions

Please check all that apply to you about the incident you identified in exercise 1.

Incident: 3

Cover

[ ] I refuse to talk about it or address it in any way to anyone—including God.

[ ] The feelings are still hurtful and thoughts and memories still vivid.

[ ] The few times I do think or talk about it, I do so in a negative manner.

[ ] It has made me bitter (untrusting or unloving toward someone) instead of better.

[ ] I have no testimony regarding it, only a sad story that I hate to share..

Conquer:

[ ] I talk about it when led to in order to help others.

[ ] The feelings are not as hurtful and thoughts and memories not as vivid.

[ ] When I talk about it, I don't demonize the person who hurt me.

[ ] It has made me better (wiser, more forgiving, more patient) instead of bitter.

[ ] It has become a testimony that I share with people in similar situations.

Have you covered or conquered this incident? Write your conclusion below:

Exercise 2 Questions

Please check all that apply to you about the incident you identified in exercise 1.

Incident: 4

Cover

[ ] I refuse to talk about it or address it in any way to anyone—including God.

[ ] The feelings are still hurtful and thoughts and memories still vivid.

[ ] The few times I do think or talk about it, I do so in a negative manner.

[ ] It has made me bitter (untrusting or unloving toward someone) instead of better.

[ ] I have no testimony regarding it, only a sad story that I hate to share..

Conquer:

[ ] I talk about it when led to in order to help others.

[ ] The feelings are not as hurtful and thoughts and memories not as vivid.

[ ] When I talk about it, I don't demonize the person who hurt me.

[ ] It has made me better (wiser, more forgiving, more patient) instead of bitter.

[ ] It has become a testimony that I share with people in similar situations.

Have you covered or conquered this incident? Write your conclusion below:

Exercise 2 Questions

Please check all that apply to you about the incident you identified in exercise 1.

Incident: 5

Cover

[ ] I refuse to talk about it or address it in any way to anyone—including God.

[ ] The feelings are still hurtful and thoughts and memories still vivid.

[ ] The few times I do think or talk about it, I do so in a negative manner.

[ ] It has made me bitter (untrusting or unloving toward someone) instead of better.

[ ] I have no testimony regarding it, only a sad story that I hate to share..

Conquer:

[ ] I talk about it when led to in order to help others.

[ ] The feelings are not as hurtful and thoughts and memories not as vivid.

[ ] When I talk about it, I don't demonize the person who hurt me.

[ ] It has made me better (wiser, more forgiving, more patient) instead of bitter.

[ ] It has become a testimony that I share with people in similar situations.

Have you covered or conquered this incident? Write your conclusion below:

Exercise 2 Questions

Please check all that apply to you about the incident you identified in exercise 1.

Incident: 6

Cover

[ ] I refuse to talk about it or address it in any way to anyone—including God.

[ ] The feelings are still hurtful and thoughts and memories still vivid.

[ ] The few times I do think or talk about it, I do so in a negative manner.

[ ] It has made me bitter (untrusting or unloving toward someone) instead of better.

[ ] I have no testimony regarding it, only a sad story that I hate to share..

Conquer:

[ ] I talk about it when led to in order to help others.

[ ] The feelings are not as hurtful and thoughts and memories not as vivid.

[ ] When I talk about it, I don't demonize the person who hurt me.

[ ] It has made me better (wiser, more forgiving, more patient) instead of bitter.

[ ] It has become a testimony that I share with people in similar situations.

Have you covered or conquered this incident? Write your conclusion below:

Exercise 2 Questions

Please check all that apply to you about the incident you identified in exercise 1.

Incident: 7

Cover

[ ] I refuse to talk about it or address it in any way to anyone—including God.

[ ] The feelings are still hurtful and thoughts and memories still vivid.

[ ] The few times I do think or talk about it, I do so in a negative manner.

[ ] It has made me bitter (untrusting or unloving toward someone) instead of better.

[ ] I have no testimony regarding it, only a sad story that I hate to share..

Conquer:

[ ] I talk about it when led to in order to help others.

[ ] The feelings are not as hurtful and thoughts and memories not as vivid.

[ ] When I talk about it, I don't demonize the person who hurt me.

[ ] It has made me better (wiser, more forgiving, more patient) instead of bitter.

[ ] It has become a testimony that I share with people in similar situations.

Have you covered or conquered this incident? Write your conclusion below:

Exercise 2 Questions

Please check all that apply to you about the incident you identified in exercise 1.

Incident: 8

Cover

[ ] I refuse to talk about it or address it in any way to anyone—including God.

[ ] The feelings are still hurtful and thoughts and memories still vivid.

[ ] The few times I do think or talk about it, I do so in a negative manner.

[ ] It has made me bitter (untrusting or unloving toward someone) instead of better.

[ ] I have no testimony regarding it, only a sad story that I hate to share..

Conquer:

[ ] I talk about it when led to in order to help others.

[ ] The feelings are not as hurtful and thoughts and memories not as vivid.

[ ] When I talk about it, I don't demonize the person who hurt me.

[ ] It has made me better (wiser, more forgiving, more patient) instead of bitter.

[ ] It has become a testimony that I share with people in similar situations.

Have you covered or conquered this incident? Write your conclusion below:

Exercise 2 Questions

Please check all that apply to you about the incident you identified in exercise 1.

Incident: 9

Cover

[ ] I refuse to talk about it or address it in any way to anyone—including God.

[ ] The feelings are still hurtful and thoughts and memories still vivid.

[ ] The few times I do think or talk about it, I do so in a negative manner.

[ ] It has made me bitter (untrusting or unloving toward someone) instead of better.

[ ] I have no testimony regarding it, only a sad story that I hate to share..

Conquer:

[ ] I talk about it when led to in order to help others.

[ ] The feelings are not as hurtful and thoughts and memories not as vivid.

[ ] When I talk about it, I don't demonize the person who hurt me.

[ ] It has made me better (wiser, more forgiving, more patient) instead of bitter.

[ ] It has become a testimony that I share with people in similar situations.

Have you covered or conquered this incident? Write your conclusion below:

Exercise 2 Questions

Please check all that apply to you about the incident you identified in exercise 1.

Incident: 10

Cover

[ ] I refuse to talk about it or address it in any way to anyone—including God.

[ ] The feelings are still hurtful and thoughts and memories still vivid.

[ ] The few times I do think or talk about it, I do so in a negative manner.

[ ] It has made me bitter (untrusting or unloving toward someone) instead of better.

[ ] I have no testimony regarding it, only a sad story that I hate to share..

Conquer:

[ ] I talk about it when led to in order to help others.

[ ] The feelings are not as hurtful and thoughts and memories not as vivid.

[ ] When I talk about it, I don't demonize the person who hurt me.

[ ] It has made me better (wiser, more forgiving, more patient) instead of bitter.

[ ] It has become a testimony that I share with people in similar situations.

Have you covered or conquered this incident? Write your conclusion below:

Exercise

3

Level Zero. Are You Here?

In the book, I share several reasons why forgiving is a stronger challenge for some. Part of it has to do with personality, how we think, and several other factors. However, regardless of any obstacles to forgiveness, we are all expected to forgive.

But what about those who may be stuck on level zero and refuse to forgive? Perhaps the emotions are too painful. Maybe the anger and hatred are overwhelming. The incident could be too fresh. The person who committed the hurt may have done so out of cold callousness—seeking to inflict as much heartache as possible.

Whatever the reason, the inability to forgive often means the inability to be healed. Holding on to anger, resentment, and hatred can result in mental, emotional, and physical problems. It is crucial to overcome and move to the next level. We do this by speaking the words of forgiveness from the heart.

But first, let's identify some obstacles that can prevent forgiveness.

Book Quotes:

"Therefore, a refusal to forgive equates to making these statements:

I refuse to forgive and be healed.

I refuse to humble myself and be exalted.

I refuse to release others from their debt and be set free.

I refuse to be obedient to God's will and be forgiven of my sins."

Exercise 3 Instructions

If possible, read chapter two in the book *The Next Level Forgiver* and answer the questions on the following pages.

If you are struggling to forgive and have not taken the first step of speaking forgiveness from the heart, I would like you to determine if any of these factors are affecting your inability to forgive. For each factor, please consult the book for how to overcome that area.

If you are sure you have forgiven, then please write how you were able to overcome and forgive.

To-Dos:

For each question, please consider going beyond merely answering and do some soul searching. Ask the deeper question of why.

Exercise 3 Questions

Incident: 1

1. I have not expressed the hurt and pain in a constructive manner. For example, I have not shared it with anyone who can give me wise advice nor revealed my real feelings and thoughts. I just don't talk about it. Is this where you are?

2. I see my sins and shortcomings as small compared to others. In other words, I constantly talk about how a person hurt me and point out everything wrong with him or her. But I rarely discuss or confess my sins and shortcomings. Does this apply to you?

3. I have not matured enough in my obedience and love for Christ. I have problems doing certain things that are difficult, including forgiving. I know I should but I don't. Is this where you are?

4. I know I need to forgive, but God knows my heart. I just need time. Is this where you are?

5. I may misunderstand forgiveness. I feel like forgiving means a person's hurtful actions against me are okay. So I choose to hold on to the anger. Is this where you are?

6. I think I have forgiven. I prayed about it and even asked God to forgive the person. Is there where you are?

7. After discussion, let's practice the first step of forgiving—saying the words.

Exercise 3 Questions

Incident: 2

1. I have not expressed the hurt and pain in a constructive manner. For example, I have not shared it with anyone who can give me wise advice nor revealed my real feelings and thoughts. I just don't talk about it. Is this where you are?

2. I see my sins and shortcomings as small compared to others. In other words, I constantly talk about how a person hurt me and point out everything wrong with him or her. But I rarely discuss or confess my sins and shortcomings. Does this apply to you?

3. I have not matured enough in my obedience and love for Christ. I have problems doing certain things that are difficult, including forgiving. I know I should but I don't. Is this where you are?

4. I know I need to forgive, but God knows my heart. I just need time. Is this where you are?

5. I may misunderstand forgiveness. I feel like forgiving means a person's hurtful actions against me are okay. So I choose to hold on to the anger. Is this where you are?

6. I think I have forgiven. I prayed about it and even asked God to forgive the person. Is there where you are?

7. After discussion, let's practice the first step of forgiving—saying the words.

Exercise 3 Questions

Incident: 3

1. I have not expressed the hurt and pain in a constructive manner. For example, I have not shared it with anyone who can give me wise advice nor revealed my real feelings and thoughts. I just don't talk about it. Is this where you are?

2. I see my sins and shortcomings as small compared to others. In other words, I constantly talk about how a person hurt me and point out everything wrong with him or her. But I rarely discuss or confess my sins and shortcomings. Does this apply to you?

3. I have not matured enough in my obedience and love for Christ. I have problems doing certain things that are difficult, including forgiving. I know I should but I don't. Is this where you are?

4. I know I need to forgive, but God knows my heart. I just need time. Is this where you are?

5. I may misunderstand forgiveness. I feel like forgiving means a person's hurtful actions against me are okay. So I choose to hold on to the anger. Is this where you are?

6. I think I have forgiven. I prayed about it and even asked God to forgive the person. Is there where you are?

7. After discussion, let's practice the first step of forgiving—saying the words.

Exercise 3 Questions

Incident: 4

1. I have not expressed the hurt and pain in a constructive manner. For example, I have not shared it with anyone who can give me wise advice nor revealed my real feelings and thoughts. I just don't talk about it. Is this where you are?

2. I see my sins and shortcomings as small compared to others. In other words, I constantly talk about how a person hurt me and point out everything wrong with him or her. But I rarely discuss or confess my sins and shortcomings. Does this apply to you?

3. I have not matured enough in my obedience and love for Christ. I have problems doing certain things that are difficult, including forgiving. I know I should but I don't. Is this where you are?

4. I know I need to forgive, but God knows my heart. I just need time. Is this where you are?

5. I may misunderstand forgiveness. I feel like forgiving means a person's hurtful actions against me are okay. So I choose to hold on to the anger. Is this where you are?

6. I think I have forgiven. I prayed about it and even asked God to forgive the person. Is there where you are?

7. After discussion, let's practice the first step of forgiving—saying the words.

Exercise 3 Questions

Incident: 5

1. I have not expressed the hurt and pain in a constructive manner. For example, I have not shared it with anyone who can give me wise advice nor revealed my real feelings and thoughts. I just don't talk about it. Is this where you are?

2. I see my sins and shortcomings as small compared to others. In other words, I constantly talk about how a person hurt me and point out everything wrong with him or her. But I rarely discuss or confess my sins and shortcomings. Does this apply to you?

3. I have not matured enough in my obedience and love for Christ. I have problems doing certain things that are difficult, including forgiving. I know I should but I don't. Is this where you are?

4. I know I need to forgive, but God knows my heart. I just need time. Is this where you are?

5. I may misunderstand forgiveness. I feel like forgiving means a person's hurtful actions against me are okay. So I choose to hold on to the anger. Is this where you are?

6. I think I have forgiven. I prayed about it and even asked God to forgive the person. Is there where you are?

7. After discussion, let's practice the first step of forgiving—saying the words.

Exercise 3 Questions

Incident: 6

1. I have not expressed the hurt and pain in a constructive manner. For example, I have not shared it with anyone who can give me wise advice nor revealed my real feelings and thoughts. I just don't talk about it. Is this where you are?

2. I see my sins and shortcomings as small compared to others. In other words, I constantly talk about how a person hurt me and point out everything wrong with him or her. But I rarely discuss or confess my sins and shortcomings. Does this apply to you?

3. I have not matured enough in my obedience and love for Christ. I have problems doing certain things that are difficult, including forgiving. I know I should but I don't. Is this where you are?

4. I know I need to forgive, but God knows my heart. I just need time. Is this where you are?

5. I may misunderstand forgiveness. I feel like forgiving means a person's hurtful actions against me are okay. So I choose to hold on to the anger. Is this where you are?

6. I think I have forgiven. I prayed about it and even asked God to forgive the person. Is there where you are?

7. After discussion, let's practice the first step of forgiving—saying the words.

Exercise 3 Questions

Incident: 7

1. I have not expressed the hurt and pain in a constructive manner. For example, I have not shared it with anyone who can give me wise advice nor revealed my real feelings and thoughts. I just don't talk about it. Is this where you are?

2. I see my sins and shortcomings as small compared to others. In other words, I constantly talk about how a person hurt me and point out everything wrong with him or her. But I rarely discuss or confess my sins and shortcomings. Does this apply to you?

3. I have not matured enough in my obedience and love for Christ. I have problems doing certain things that are difficult, including forgiving. I know I should but I don't. Is this where you are?

4. I know I need to forgive, but God knows my heart. I just need time. Is this where you are?

5. I may misunderstand forgiveness. I feel like forgiving means a person's hurtful actions against me are okay. So I choose to hold on to the anger. Is this where you are?

6. I think I have forgiven. I prayed about it and even asked God to forgive the person. Is there where you are?

7. After discussion, let's practice the first step of forgiving—saying the words.

Exercise 3 Questions

Incident: 8

1. I have not expressed the hurt and pain in a constructive manner. For example, I have not shared it with anyone who can give me wise advice nor revealed my real feelings and thoughts. I just don't talk about it. Is this where you are?

2. I see my sins and shortcomings as small compared to others. In other words, I constantly talk about how a person hurt me and point out everything wrong with him or her. But I rarely discuss or confess my sins and shortcomings. Does this apply to you?

3. I have not matured enough in my obedience and love for Christ. I have problems doing certain things that are difficult, including forgiving. I know I should but I don't. Is this where you are?

4. I know I need to forgive, but God knows my heart. I just need time. Is this where you are?

5. I may misunderstand forgiveness. I feel like forgiving means a person's hurtful actions against me are okay. So I choose to hold on to the anger. Is this where you are?

6. I think I have forgiven. I prayed about it and even asked God to forgive the person. Is there where you are?

7. After discussion, let's practice the first step of forgiving—saying the words.

Exercise 3 Questions

Incident: 9

1. I have not expressed the hurt and pain in a constructive manner. For example, I have not shared it with anyone who can give me wise advice nor revealed my real feelings and thoughts. I just don't talk about it. Is this where you are?

2. I see my sins and shortcomings as small compared to others. In other words, I constantly talk about how a person hurt me and point out everything wrong with him or her. But I rarely discuss or confess my sins and shortcomings. Does this apply to you?

3. I have not matured enough in my obedience and love for Christ. I have problems doing certain things that are difficult, including forgiving. I know I should but I don't. Is this where you are?

4. I know I need to forgive, but God knows my heart. I just need time. Is this where you are?

5. I may misunderstand forgiveness. I feel like forgiving means a person's hurtful actions against me are okay. So I choose to hold on to the anger. Is this where you are?

6. I think I have forgiven. I prayed about it and even asked God to forgive the person. Is there where you are?

7. After discussion, let's practice the first step of forgiving—saying the words.

Exercise 3 Questions

Incident: 10

1. I have not expressed the hurt and pain in a constructive manner. For example, I have not shared it with anyone who can give me wise advice nor revealed my real feelings and thoughts. I just don't talk about it. Is this where you are?

2. I see my sins and shortcomings as small compared to others. In other words, I constantly talk about how a person hurt me and point out everything wrong with him or her. But I rarely discuss or confess my sins and shortcomings. Does this apply to you?

3. I have not matured enough in my obedience and love for Christ. I have problems doing certain things that are difficult, including forgiving. I know I should but I don't. Is this where you are?

4. I know I need to forgive, but God knows my heart. I just need time. Is this where you are?

5. I may misunderstand forgiveness. I feel like forgiving means a person's hurtful actions against me are okay. So I choose to hold on to the anger. Is this where you are?

6. I think I have forgiven. I prayed about it and even asked God to forgive the person. Is there where you are?

7. After discussion, let's practice the first step of forgiving—saying the words.

EXERCISE

4

LEVEL ONE. ARE YOU HERE?

If you had an issue with forgiving, you hopefully found the strength from the last exercise to say the words *I forgive*.

Speaking the words is a first step, but accomplishing this does not remove the hurtful emotions, negative thoughts, or invisible wall between individuals.

If this describes your situation, more than likely you may have said, "I forgive, but I'm done with that person." Do you have or have you had one of those relationships? The broken type where you vowed to never trust, believe, or come close to a person?

In this exercise, we will determine the existence of a barrier between you and another person, if it's justified, and how to overcome it.

Book Quotes:

"Have you ever extended someone conditional forgiveness as I did with God? In other words, I said, 'Lord, I forgive You, but our relationship will never be the same.'

How arrogant of me. Fortunately, God doesn't take every word we say seriously. He knows when we speak from hurt and bitterness and offers grace and mercy instead of instant judgment."

"Have you ever spoken the words of forgiveness yet pushed someone completely out of your life—vowing never to love or trust that person again? Do you have an estranged relationship that needs to be repaired?"

Exercise 4 Instructions

If possible, read chapter three in the book *The Next Level Forgiver* before doing this exercise.

For each incident you identified in exercise 1, answer the questions on the following pages.

Please be as open and honest as possible. It's okay to be unsure. The purpose of these questions is to stimulate thought and discussion that lead to answers and understanding.

To Dos:

Write a short letter to the person who hurt you and express your emotions. Read it to yourself a few times. You can give it to the person or destroy it.

Exercise 4 Questions

Incident: 1

1. Have you forgiven the person(s) involved in this incident?

2. Is this person(s) still alive?

3. Was there or is there a barrier between you and the person(s)?

   Indicators of barriers:

   - I'm not comfortable around the person.

   - A person's presence causes me to constantly think about the hurt.

   - Our conversation is not the same as before the incident.

   - I don't enjoy being with the person.

   - I never say anything positive about the person, only negative.

4. Is this a justified barrier? Is there a good reason to keep the wall in place?

   Some justified reasons:

   - Violent crime

   - Abuse (physical, verbal, or emotional)

   - A person who continues to perpetrate hurt and pain

   - Other (if you have another reason, write it here):

5. Is this an unjustified barrier? Is it something that should be removed and relationship restored?

   - Some unjustified reasons:

   - The person knows the hurt and is sorry, though he/she may not have apologized.

   - There was a good relationship, and the incident tore it apart.

   - There was never a good relationship, but there should be and is worth pursuing.

6. If the barrier is unjustified and should be removed, what is your next step?

Exercise 4 Questions

Incident: 2

1. Have you forgiven the person(s) involved in this incident?

2. Is this person(s) still alive?

3. Was there or is there a barrier between you and the person(s)?

    Indicators of barriers:

    - I'm not comfortable around the person.

    - A person's presence causes me to constantly think about the hurt.

    - Our conversation is not the same as before the incident.

    - I don't enjoy being with the person.

    - I never say anything positive about the person, only negative.

4. Is this a justified barrier? Is there a good reason to keep the wall in place?

    Some justified reasons:

    - Violent crime

    - Abuse (physical, verbal, or emotional)

    - A person who continues to perpetrate hurt and pain

    - Other (if you have another reason, write it here):

5. Is this an unjustified barrier? Is it something that should be removed and relationship restored?

    - Some unjustified reasons:

    - The person knows the hurt and is sorry, though he/she may not have apologized.

    - There was a good relationship, and the incident tore it apart.

    - There was never a good relationship, but there should be and is worth pursuing.

6. If the barrier is unjustified and should be removed, what is your next step?

Exercise 4 Questions

Incident: 3

1. Have you forgiven the person(s) involved in this incident?

2. Is this person(s) still alive?

3. Was there or is there a barrier between you and the person(s)?

   Indicators of barriers:

   - I'm not comfortable around the person.

   - A person's presence causes me to constantly think about the hurt.

   - Our conversation is not the same as before the incident.

   - I don't enjoy being with the person.

   - I never say anything positive about the person, only negative.

4. Is this a justified barrier? Is there a good reason to keep the wall in place?

   Some justified reasons:

   - Violent crime

   - Abuse (physical, verbal, or emotional)

   - A person who continues to perpetrate hurt and pain

   - Other (if you have another reason, write it here):

5. Is this an unjustified barrier? Is it something that should be removed and relationship restored?

   - Some unjustified reasons:

   - The person knows the hurt and is sorry, though he/she may not have apologized.

   - There was a good relationship, and the incident tore it apart.

   - There was never a good relationship, but there should be and is worth pursuing.

6. If the barrier is unjustified and should be removed, what is your next step?

Exercise 4 Questions

Incident: 4

1. Have you forgiven the person(s) involved in this incident?

2. Is this person(s) still alive?

3. Was there or is there a barrier between you and the person(s)?

   Indicators of barriers:

   - I'm not comfortable around the person.

   - A person's presence causes me to constantly think about the hurt.

   - Our conversation is not the same as before the incident.

   - I don't enjoy being with the person.

   - I never say anything positive about the person, only negative.

4. Is this a justified barrier? Is there a good reason to keep the wall in place?

   Some justified reasons:

   - Violent crime

   - Abuse (physical, verbal, or emotional)

   - A person who continues to perpetrate hurt and pain

   - Other (if you have another reason, write it here):

5. Is this an unjustified barrier? Is it something that should be removed and relationship restored?

   - Some unjustified reasons:

   - The person knows the hurt and is sorry, though he/she may not have apologized.

   - There was a good relationship, and the incident tore it apart.

   - There was never a good relationship, but there should be and is worth pursuing.

6. If the barrier is unjustified and should be removed, what is your next step?

Exercise 4 Questions

Incident: 5

1. Have you forgiven the person(s) involved in this incident?

2. Is this person(s) still alive?

3. Was there or is there a barrier between you and the person(s)?

   Indicators of barriers:

   - I'm not comfortable around the person.

   - A person's presence causes me to constantly think about the hurt.

   - Our conversation is not the same as before the incident.

   - I don't enjoy being with the person.

   - I never say anything positive about the person, only negative.

4. Is this a justified barrier? Is there a good reason to keep the wall in place?

   Some justified reasons:

   - Violent crime

   - Abuse (physical, verbal, or emotional)

   - A person who continues to perpetrate hurt and pain

   - Other (if you have another reason, write it here):

5. Is this an unjustified barrier? Is it something that should be removed and relationship restored?

   - Some unjustified reasons:

   - The person knows the hurt and is sorry, though he/she may not have apologized.

   - There was a good relationship, and the incident tore it apart.

   - There was never a good relationship, but there should be and is worth pursuing.

6. If the barrier is unjustified and should be removed, what is your next step?

Exercise 4 Questions

Incident: 6

1. Have you forgiven the person(s) involved in this incident?

2. Is this person(s) still alive?

3. Was there or is there a barrier between you and the person(s)?

   Indicators of barriers:

   - I'm not comfortable around the person.

   - A person's presence causes me to constantly think about the hurt.

   - Our conversation is not the same as before the incident.

   - I don't enjoy being with the person.

   - I never say anything positive about the person, only negative.

4. Is this a justified barrier? Is there a good reason to keep the wall in place?

   Some justified reasons:

   - Violent crime

   - Abuse (physical, verbal, or emotional)

   - A person who continues to perpetrate hurt and pain

   - Other (if you have another reason, write it here):

5. Is this an unjustified barrier? Is it something that should be removed and relationship restored?

   - Some unjustified reasons:

   - The person knows the hurt and is sorry, though he/she may not have apologized.

   - There was a good relationship, and the incident tore it apart.

   - There was never a good relationship, but there should be and is worth pursuing.

6. If the barrier is unjustified and should be removed, what is your next step?

Exercise 4 Questions

Incident: 7

1. Have you forgiven the person(s) involved in this incident?

2. Is this person(s) still alive?

3. Was there or is there a barrier between you and the person(s)?

    Indicators of barriers:

    - I'm not comfortable around the person.

    - A person's presence causes me to constantly think about the hurt.

    - Our conversation is not the same as before the incident.

    - I don't enjoy being with the person.

    - I never say anything positive about the person, only negative.

4. Is this a justified barrier? Is there a good reason to keep the wall in place?

    Some justified reasons:

    - Violent crime

    - Abuse (physical, verbal, or emotional)

    - A person who continues to perpetrate hurt and pain

    - Other (if you have another reason, write it here):

5. Is this an unjustified barrier? Is it something that should be removed and relationship restored?

    - Some unjustified reasons:

    - The person knows the hurt and is sorry, though he/she may not have apologized.

    - There was a good relationship, and the incident tore it apart.

    - There was never a good relationship, but there should be and is worth pursuing.

6. If the barrier is unjustified and should be removed, what is your next step?

Exercise 4 Questions

Incident: 8

1. Have you forgiven the person(s) involved in this incident?

2. Is this person(s) still alive?

3. Was there or is there a barrier between you and the person(s)?

    Indicators of barriers:

    - I'm not comfortable around the person.

    - A person's presence causes me to constantly think about the hurt.

    - Our conversation is not the same as before the incident.

    - I don't enjoy being with the person.

    - I never say anything positive about the person, only negative.

4. Is this a justified barrier? Is there a good reason to keep the wall in place?

    Some justified reasons:

    - Violent crime

    - Abuse (physical, verbal, or emotional)

    - A person who continues to perpetrate hurt and pain

    - Other (if you have another reason, write it here):

5. Is this an unjustified barrier? Is it something that should be removed and relationship restored?

    - Some unjustified reasons:

    - The person knows the hurt and is sorry, though he/she may not have apologized.

    - There was a good relationship, and the incident tore it apart.

    - There was never a good relationship, but there should be and is worth pursuing.

6. If the barrier is unjustified and should be removed, what is your next step?

Exercise 4 Questions

Incident: 9

1. Have you forgiven the person(s) involved in this incident?

2. Is this person(s) still alive?

3. Was there or is there a barrier between you and the person(s)?

    Indicators of barriers:

    - I'm not comfortable around the person.

    - A person's presence causes me to constantly think about the hurt.

    - Our conversation is not the same as before the incident.

    - I don't enjoy being with the person.

    - I never say anything positive about the person, only negative.

4. Is this a justified barrier? Is there a good reason to keep the wall in place?

    Some justified reasons:

    - Violent crime

    - Abuse (physical, verbal, or emotional)

    - A person who continues to perpetrate hurt and pain

    - Other (if you have another reason, write it here):

5. Is this an unjustified barrier? Is it something that should be removed and relationship restored?

    - Some unjustified reasons:

    - The person knows the hurt and is sorry, though he/she may not have apologized.

    - There was a good relationship, and the incident tore it apart.

    - There was never a good relationship, but there should be and is worth pursuing.

6. If the barrier is unjustified and should be removed, what is your next step?

Exercise 4 Questions

Incident: 10

1. Have you forgiven the person(s) involved in this incident?

2. Is this person(s) still alive?

3. Was there or is there a barrier between you and the person(s)?

   Indicators of barriers:

   - I'm not comfortable around the person.

   - A person's presence causes me to constantly think about the hurt.

   - Our conversation is not the same as before the incident.

   - I don't enjoy being with the person.

   - I never say anything positive about the person, only negative.

4. Is this a justified barrier? Is there a good reason to keep the wall in place?

   Some justified reasons:

   - Violent crime

   - Abuse (physical, verbal, or emotional)

   - A person who continues to perpetrate hurt and pain

   - Other (if you have another reason, write it here):

5. Is this an unjustified barrier? Is it something that should be removed and relationship restored?

   - Some unjustified reasons:

   - The person knows the hurt and is sorry, though he/she may not have apologized.

   - There was a good relationship, and the incident tore it apart.

   - There was never a good relationship, but there should be and is worth pursuing.

6. If the barrier is unjustified and should be removed, what is your next step?

Exercise

5

Level Two. Are You Here?

If you've moved to level two forgiveness, you understand your perpetrator should not be condemned but assisted. Therefore, you've offered up prayers for that person to be saved, changed, or even convicted of their wrongs.

But praying for someone is much easier than praying with the person. That way, you don't have eye contact. You don't hear his or her voice. You don't feel the person's presence. And you don't have to pretend what he or she has said or did doesn't hurt. It is difficult to face someone who heaped pain on you.

In your situation, there may be an invisible wall of separation that should come down.

Let's assume you've completed the previous exercise and have determined you have broken relationships worth restoring. Now what? How do you go about seeking to restore something lost long ago?

I suggest you see things in a broader sense. While restoration of the relationship should be a goal, it should not be the only aim. I believe there is a greater lesson your perpetrator can learn about the love, forgiveness, and grace of Jesus Christ demonstrated through you.

Book Quotes:

"Step three: Interact with the person. This could be, depending on the offense, the most difficult step to accomplish. As mentioned in previous chapters, care and wisdom should be taken when interacting with individuals under certain circumstances. Be wise with whom you interact and how it takes place but be passionate in your pursuit of relationships that should be restored."

Exercise 5 Instructions

If possible, read chapter four in the book *The Next Level Forgiver* before doing this exercise.

For each incident you identified in exercise 1, answer the questions on the following pages.

Please be as open and honest as possible. It's okay to be unsure. The purpose of these questions is to stimulate thought and discussion that lead to answers and understanding.

To Dos:

Write a few reasons why some or all of your broken relationships should be restored.

Pretend you are about to see that person for the last time and you have a brief minute to tell him or her something. What would that something be?

Exercise 5 Questions

Incident: 1

1. If you reached out to this person, what do you think his or her reaction would be?

2. Think about your reaction to what was done or said. Did you react in a godly manner? If not, that may a good starting place—to apologize for an ungodly reaction.

3. If you were practicing in a mirror some words to say to that person, what would you say? Write it here.

4. If that person knows you were hurt by something he or she did, have you told him or her that you forgive? If not, why not?

5. Determine a date, time, and method to reach out to him or her. Pray for words to say. Follow up and reach out. Write the results below.

6. Did the person respond favorably or unfavorably? Write their reactions below.

7. Afterwards, how did reaching out make you feel?

Exercise 5 Questions

Incident: 2

1. If you reached out to this person, what do you think his or her reaction would be?

2. Think about your reaction to what was done or said. Did you react in a godly manner? If not, that may a good starting place—to apologize for an ungodly reaction.

3. If you were practicing in a mirror some words to say to that person, what would you say? Write it here.

4. If that person knows you were hurt by something he or she did, have you told him or her that you forgive? If not, why not?

5. Determine a date, time, and method to reach out to him or her. Pray for words to say. Follow up and reach out. Write the results below.

6. Did the person respond favorably or unfavorably? Write their reactions below.

7. Afterwards, how did reaching out make you feel?

Exercise 5 Questions

Incident: 3

1. If you reached out to this person, what do you think his or her reaction would be?

2. Think about your reaction to what was done or said. Did you react in a godly manner? If not, that may a good starting place—to apologize for an ungodly reaction.

3. If you were practicing in a mirror some words to say to that person, what would you say? Write it here.

4. If that person knows you were hurt by something he or she did, have you told him or her that you forgive? If not, why not?

5. Determine a date, time, and method to reach out to him or her. Pray for words to say. Follow up and reach out. Write the results below.

6. Did the person respond favorably or unfavorably? Write their reactions below.

7. Afterwards, how did reaching out make you feel?

THE NEXT LEVEL FORGIVER WORK BOOKLET

Exercise 5 Questions

Incident: 4

1. If you reached out to this person, what do you think his or her reaction would be?

2. Think about your reaction to what was done or said. Did you react in a godly manner? If not, that may a good starting place—to apologize for an ungodly reaction.

3. If you were practicing in a mirror some words to say to that person, what would you say? Write it here.

4. If that person knows you were hurt by something he or she did, have you told him or her that you forgive? If not, why not?

5. Determine a date, time, and method to reach out to him or her. Pray for words to say. Follow up and reach out. Write the results below.

6. Did the person respond favorably or unfavorably? Write their reactions below.

7. Afterwards, how did reaching out make you feel?

Exercise 5 Questions

Incident: 5

1. If you reached out to this person, what do you think his or her reaction would be?

2. Think about your reaction to what was done or said. Did you react in a godly manner? If not, that may a good starting place—to apologize for an ungodly reaction.

3. If you were practicing in a mirror some words to say to that person, what would you say? Write it here.

4. If that person knows you were hurt by something he or she did, have you told him or her that you forgive? If not, why not?

5. Determine a date, time, and method to reach out to him or her. Pray for words to say. Follow up and reach out. Write the results below.

6. Did the person respond favorably or unfavorably? Write their reactions below.

7. Afterwards, how did reaching out make you feel?

Exercise 5 Questions

Incident: 6

1. If you reached out to this person, what do you think his or her reaction would be?

2. Think about your reaction to what was done or said. Did you react in a godly manner? If not, that may a good starting place—to apologize for an ungodly reaction.

3. If you were practicing in a mirror some words to say to that person, what would you say? Write it here.

4. If that person knows you were hurt by something he or she did, have you told him or her that you forgive? If not, why not?

5. Determine a date, time, and method to reach out to him or her. Pray for words to say. Follow up and reach out. Write the results below.

6. Did the person respond favorably or unfavorably? Write their reactions below.

7. Afterwards, how did reaching out make you feel?

Exercise 5 Questions

Incident: 7

1. If you reached out to this person, what do you think his or her reaction would be?

2. Think about your reaction to what was done or said. Did you react in a godly manner? If not, that may a good starting place—to apologize for an ungodly reaction.

3. If you were practicing in a mirror some words to say to that person, what would you say? Write it here.

4. If that person knows you were hurt by something he or she did, have you told him or her that you forgive? If not, why not?

5. Determine a date, time, and method to reach out to him or her. Pray for words to say. Follow up and reach out. Write the results below.

6. Did the person respond favorably or unfavorably? Write their reactions below.

7. Afterwards, how did reaching out make you feel?

Exercise 5 Questions

Incident: 8

1. If you reached out to this person, what do you think his or her reaction would be?

2. Think about your reaction to what was done or said. Did you react in a godly manner? If not, that may a good starting place—to apologize for an ungodly reaction.

3. If you were practicing in a mirror some words to say to that person, what would you say? Write it here.

4. If that person knows you were hurt by something he or she did, have you told him or her that you forgive? If not, why not?

5. Determine a date, time, and method to reach out to him or her. Pray for words to say. Follow up and reach out. Write the results below.

6. Did the person respond favorably or unfavorably? Write their reactions below.

7. Afterwards, how did reaching out make you feel?

Exercise 5 Questions

Incident: 9

1. If you reached out to this person, what do you think his or her reaction would be?

2. Think about your reaction to what was done or said. Did you react in a godly manner? If not, that may a good starting place—to apologize for an ungodly reaction.

3. If you were practicing in a mirror some words to say to that person, what would you say? Write it here.

4. If that person knows you were hurt by something he or she did, have you told him or her that you forgive? If not, why not?

5. Determine a date, time, and method to reach out to him or her. Pray for words to say. Follow up and reach out. Write the results below.

6. Did the person respond favorably or unfavorably? Write their reactions below.

7. Afterwards, how did reaching out make you feel?

Exercise 5 Questions

Incident: 10

1. If you reached out to this person, what do you think his or her reaction would be?

2. Think about your reaction to what was done or said. Did you react in a godly manner? If not, that may a good starting place—to apologize for an ungodly reaction.

3. If you were practicing in a mirror some words to say to that person, what would you say? Write it here.

4. If that person knows you were hurt by something he or she did, have you told him or her that you forgive? If not, why not?

5. Determine a date, time, and method to reach out to him or her. Pray for words to say. Follow up and reach out. Write the results below.

6. Did the person respond favorably or unfavorably? Write their reactions below.

7. Afterwards, how did reaching out make you feel?

EXERCISE

6

LEVEL THREE. AM I HERE?

I believe this exercise will be the most challenging. Level three forgiveness involves, if applicable, making contact and interacting with the person who hurt you.

You will have to endure the memories, fight the emotional swings, and resist the mental suggestion to forgo this process. You must make the determination to act within the will and ways of God despite inclinations to do the opposite. There will be a tremendous battle between your spiritual will and emotional will. Which one will rule?

As you seek to follow this exercise, please use wisdom when interacting with the person. Do not put yourself in harm or danger. If you feel interaction is necessary but physical interaction may be unwise, consider other options such as writing, calling, or even social media contact.

Always remember the goals of facing a person: to lead him or her into repentance, to release your burden, and to restore or introduce the person to God.

Book Quotes

"The person who raped or molested you has greater in him. The trusted friend who betrayed you should not be equated to his or her act of betrayal. The person who senselessly murdered your loved one committed a horrible act that turned your life upside down, but even that person was created for greater by God. Thus, the Lord continues His pursuit, even of those who have carried out horrific acts.."

Exercise 6 Instructions

If possible, read chapter five in the book *The Next Level Forgiver* before doing this exercise.

For each incident you identified in exercise 1, answer the questions on the following pages.

Please be as open and honest as possible. It's okay to be unsure. The purpose of these questions is to stimulate thought and discussion that lead to answers and understanding.

To Dos:

If applicable, write down some ways of reaching out to the person. Form a plan and follow it.

Exercise 6 Questions

Incident: 1

1. Have you spoken the words of forgiveness?

2. Have you prayed for the person(s)?

3. If applicable, have you removed the invisible barrier by telling the person you forgive him or her?

4. If applicable, have you accepted opportunities to help the person?

5. Have you sought opportunities to witness to the person?

6. If you've had encounters with this person, write what happened.

7. If you are struggling with interacting with this person, write about the areas you struggle with.

Exercise 6 Questions

Incident: 2

1. Have you spoken the words of forgiveness?

2. Have you prayed for the person(s)?

3. If applicable, have you removed the invisible barrier by telling the person you forgive him or her?

4. If applicable, have you accepted opportunities to help the person?

5. Have you sought opportunities to witness to the person?

6. If you've had encounters with this person, write what happened.

7. If you are struggling with interacting with this person, write about the areas you struggle with.

Exercise 6 Questions

Incident: 3

1. Have you spoken the words of forgiveness?

2. Have you prayed for the person(s)?

3. If applicable, have you removed the invisible barrier by telling the person you forgive him or her?

4. If applicable, have you accepted opportunities to help the person?

5. Have you sought opportunities to witness to the person?

6. If you've had encounters with this person, write what happened.

7. If you are struggling with interacting with this person, write about the areas you struggle with.

Exercise 6 Questions

Incident: 4

1. Have you spoken the words of forgiveness?

2. Have you prayed for the person(s)?

3. If applicable, have you removed the invisible barrier by telling the person you forgive him or her?

4. If applicable, have you accepted opportunities to help the person?

5. Have you sought opportunities to witness to the person?

6. If you've had encounters with this person, write what happened.

7. If you are struggling with interacting with this person, write about the areas you struggle with.

Exercise 6 Questions

Incident: 5

1. Have you spoken the words of forgiveness?

2. Have you prayed for the person(s)?

3. If applicable, have you removed the invisible barrier by telling the person you forgive him or her?

4. If applicable, have you accepted opportunities to help the person?

5. Have you sought opportunities to witness to the person?

6. If you've had encounters with this person, write what happened.

7. If you are struggling with interacting with this person, write about the areas you struggle with.

Exercise 6 Questions

Incident: 6

1. Have you spoken the words of forgiveness?

2. Have you prayed for the person(s)?

3. If applicable, have you removed the invisible barrier by telling the person you forgive him or her?

4. If applicable, have you accepted opportunities to help the person?

5. Have you sought opportunities to witness to the person?

6. If you've had encounters with this person, write what happened.

7. If you are struggling with interacting with this person, write about the areas you struggle with.

Exercise 6 Questions

Incident: 7

1. Have you spoken the words of forgiveness?

2. Have you prayed for the person(s)?

3. If applicable, have you removed the invisible barrier by telling the person you forgive him or her?

4. If applicable, have you accepted opportunities to help the person?

5. Have you sought opportunities to witness to the person?

6. If you've had encounters with this person, write what happened.

7. If you are struggling with interacting with this person, write about the areas you struggle with.

Exercise 6 Questions

Incident: 8

1. Have you spoken the words of forgiveness?

2. Have you prayed for the person(s)?

3. If applicable, have you removed the invisible barrier by telling the person you forgive him or her?

4. If applicable, have you accepted opportunities to help the person?

5. Have you sought opportunities to witness to the person?

6. If you've had encounters with this person, write what happened.

7. If you are struggling with interacting with this person, write about the areas you struggle with.

Exercise 6 Questions

Incident: 9

1. Have you spoken the words of forgiveness?

2. Have you prayed for the person(s)?

3. If applicable, have you removed the invisible barrier by telling the person you forgive him or her?

4. If applicable, have you accepted opportunities to help the person?

5. Have you sought opportunities to witness to the person?

6. If you've had encounters with this person, write what happened.

7. If you are struggling with interacting with this person, write about the areas you struggle with.

Exercise 6 Questions

Incident: 10

1. Have you spoken the words of forgiveness?

2. Have you prayed for the person(s)?

3. If applicable, have you removed the invisible barrier by telling the person you forgive him or her?

4. If applicable, have you accepted opportunities to help the person?

5. Have you sought opportunities to witness to the person?

6. If you've had encounters with this person, write what happened.

7. If you are struggling with interacting with this person, write about the areas you struggle with.

Exercise

7

Have You Adopted Postures and Practiced Principles?

Postures (Details in chapter six of the book)

I will adopt the postures below and stand with an:

> **Open Mind:** I am aware people will hurt me.
>
> **Open Eyes:** I see beyond a person's faults and into his or her needs.
>
> **Open Mouth:** I am prepared to say "I forgive you."
>
> **Open Heart:** I give others room to hurt me.
>
> **Open Arms:** I stand ready to invite anyone back into my life.

Principles (Details in chapter six of the book)

I will practice the principles below and will not:

> **Hurt** the person physically, mentally, or emotionally.
>
> **Scandalize** the person's name by spreading negative information.
>
> **Rehash** what a person did to me or use it to deny him or her assistance.
>
> **Separate** myself from a person unless there is a good reason.

Exercise 7 Instructions

If possible, read chapter six in the book *The Next Level Forgiver* before doing this exercise.

For each incident you identified in exercise 1, answer the questions on the following pages.

Please be as open and honest as possible. It's okay to be unsure. The purpose of these questions is to stimulate thought and discussion that lead to answers and understanding.

To Dos:

Memorize the postures and principles well enough to write them.

Make notes about the things you find difficult. Why do you think those things are hard? What will help you overcome?

Exercise 7 Questions

Incident: 1

1. Do you have an:

   Open Mind: Are you aware people will hurt you?

   Open Eyes: Do you see beyond a person's faults and into his or her needs?

   Open Mouth: Are you prepared to say, "I forgive you?"

   Open Heart: Do you give others room to hurt you?

   Open Arms: Do you stand ready to invite anyone back into your life?

2. Have you practiced the principles and agree not to:

   Hurt the person physically, mentally, or emotionally?

   Scandalize the person's name by spreading negative information?

   Rehash what a person did or use it to deny assistance?

   Separate yourself from a person unless there is a reason?

Exercise 7 Questions

Incident: 2

1. Do you have an:

   Open Mind: Are you aware people will hurt you?

   Open Eyes: Do you see beyond a person's faults and into his or her needs?

   Open Mouth: Are you prepared to say, "I forgive you?"

   Open Heart: Do you give others room to hurt you?

   Open Arms: Do you stand ready to invite anyone back into your life?

2. Have you practiced the principles and agree not to:

   Hurt the person physically, mentally, or emotionally?

   Scandalize the person's name by spreading negative information?

   Rehash what a person did or use it to deny assistance?

   Separate yourself from a person unless there is a reason?

Exercise 7 Questions

Incident: 3

1. Do you have an:

   Open Mind: Are you aware people will hurt you?

   Open Eyes: Do you see beyond a person's faults and into his or her needs?

   Open Mouth: Are you prepared to say, "I forgive you?"

   Open Heart: Do you give others room to hurt you?

   Open Arms: Do you stand ready to invite anyone back into your life?

2. Have you practiced the principles and agree not to:

   Hurt the person physically, mentally, or emotionally?

   Scandalize the person's name by spreading negative information?

   Rehash what a person did or use it to deny assistance?

   Separate yourself from a person unless there is a reason?

Exercise 7 Questions

Incident: 4

1. Do you have an:

    Open Mind: Are you aware people will hurt you?

    Open Eyes: Do you see beyond a person's faults and into his or her needs?

    Open Mouth: Are you prepared to say, "I forgive you?"

    Open Heart: Do you give others room to hurt you?

    Open Arms: Do you stand ready to invite anyone back into your life?

2. Have you practiced the principles and agree not to:

    Hurt the person physically, mentally, or emotionally?

    Scandalize the person's name by spreading negative information?

    Rehash what a person did or use it to deny assistance?

    Separate yourself from a person unless there is a reason?

Exercise 7 Questions

Incident: 5

1. Do you have an:

   Open Mind: Are you aware people will hurt you?

   Open Eyes: Do you see beyond a person's faults and into his or her needs?

   Open Mouth: Are you prepared to say, "I forgive you?"

   Open Heart: Do you give others room to hurt you?

   Open Arms: Do you stand ready to invite anyone back into your life?

2. Have you practiced the principles and agree not to:

   Hurt the person physically, mentally, or emotionally?

   Scandalize the person's name by spreading negative information?

   Rehash what a person did or use it to deny assistance?

   Separate yourself from a person unless there is a reason?

Exercise 7 Questions

Incident: 6

1. Do you have an:

    Open Mind: Are you aware people will hurt you?

    Open Eyes: Do you see beyond a person's faults and into his or her needs?

    Open Mouth: Are you prepared to say, "I forgive you?"

    Open Heart: Do you give others room to hurt you?

    Open Arms: Do you stand ready to invite anyone back into your life?

2. Have you practiced the principles and agree not to:

    Hurt the person physically, mentally, or emotionally?

    Scandalize the person's name by spreading negative information?

    Rehash what a person did or use it to deny assistance?

    Separate yourself from a person unless there is a reason?

Exercise 7 Questions

Incident: 7

1. Do you have an:

   Open Mind: Are you aware people will hurt you?

   Open Eyes: Do you see beyond a person's faults and into his or her needs?

   Open Mouth: Are you prepared to say, "I forgive you?"

   Open Heart: Do you give others room to hurt you?

   Open Arms: Do you stand ready to invite anyone back into your life?

2. Have you practiced the principles and agree not to:

   Hurt the person physically, mentally, or emotionally?

   Scandalize the person's name by spreading negative information?

   Rehash what a person did or use it to deny assistance?

   Separate yourself from a person unless there is a reason?

Exercise 7 Questions

Incident: 8

1. Do you have an:

   Open Mind: Are you aware people will hurt you?

   Open Eyes: Do you see beyond a person's faults and into his or her needs?

   Open Mouth: Are you prepared to say, "I forgive you?"

   Open Heart: Do you give others room to hurt you?

   Open Arms: Do you stand ready to invite anyone back into your life?

2. Have you practiced the principles and agree not to:

   Hurt the person physically, mentally, or emotionally?

   Scandalize the person's name by spreading negative information?

   Rehash what a person did or use it to deny assistance?

   Separate yourself from a person unless there is a reason?

Exercise 7 Questions

Incident: 9

1. Do you have an:

    Open Mind: Are you aware people will hurt you?

    Open Eyes: Do you see beyond a person's faults and into his or her needs?

    Open Mouth: Are you prepared to say, "I forgive you?"

    Open Heart: Do you give others room to hurt you?

    Open Arms: Do you stand ready to invite anyone back into your life?

2. Have you practiced the principles and agree not to:

    Hurt the person physically, mentally, or emotionally?

    Scandalize the person's name by spreading negative information?

    Rehash what a person did or use it to deny assistance?

    Separate yourself from a person unless there is a reason?

Exercise 7 Questions

Incident: 10

1. Do you have an:

    Open Mind: Are you aware people will hurt you?

    Open Eyes: Do you see beyond a person's faults and into his or her needs?

    Open Mouth: Are you prepared to say, "I forgive you?"

    Open Heart: Do you give others room to hurt you?

    Open Arms: Do you stand ready to invite anyone back into your life?

2. Have you practiced the principles and agree not to:

    Hurt the person physically, mentally, or emotionally?

    Scandalize the person's name by spreading negative information?

    Rehash what a person did or use it to deny assistance?

    Separate yourself from a person unless there is a reason?

Exercise

8

Have You Forgiven Persecution?

Have you experienced severe persecution such as:

- Physical attacks, including attempts to kill?

- Rape or sexual assault?

- Stolen or destroyed property?

- Torture or the murder of loved ones?

As mentioned in the book, persecution can be very difficult to forgive. The long road to peace is often lined with obstacles of deep hurt and pain. But with the help of God, all things are possible.

Book quotes:

"If you have experienced persecution or know someone who has, do you think it's possible to walk on level three forgiveness? The process of forgiving may be much harder due to the depth of physical, mental, and emotional pain—but it is possible.

According to the Christian faith, there is no limit to what should be forgiven between individuals. No matter how hurtful or humiliating the offense, the Lord Jesus Christ instructs and expects His followers to forgive. But because He knows our deepest fears and pains, He is patient and gives supernatural assistance during the long and challenging journey to forgive."

Exercise 8 Instructions

If possible, read chapter seven in the book *The Next Level Forgiver* before doing this exercise.

For each incident you identified in exercise 1, answer the questions on the following pages.

Please be as open and honest as possible. It's okay to be unsure. The purpose of these questions is to stimulate thought and discussion that lead to answers and understanding.

To Dos:

Make notes on why you should forgive or how you forgave something as horrible as persecution.

Exercise 8 Questions

Incident: 1

1. Have you expressed the hurt? Have you shared it with anyone?

2. Do you realize how it has affected you emotionally and mentally?

3. Do you still struggle with memories of the incident?

4. Which emotions come with the painful memories?

Anger

Hatred

Sadness

Depression

Fear

Sorrow

Other:

5. Do you realize who the enemy really is?

6. Have you taken the steps of forgiveness in the book? Why or why not?

7. What areas are you struggling with?

Speaking the words of forgiveness

Seeing the person as a person in need

Experiencing haunting nightmares of what happened

Overcoming hatred for the person

Other:

Exercise 8 Questions

Incident: 2

1. Have you expressed the hurt? Have you shared it with anyone?

2. Do you realize how it has affected you emotionally and mentally?

3. Do you still struggle with memories of the incident?

4. Which emotions come with the painful memories?
Anger

Hatred

Sadness

Depression

Fear

Sorrow

Other:

5. Do you realize who the enemy really is?

6. Have you taken the steps of forgiveness in the book? Why or why not?

7. What areas are you struggling with?
Speaking the words of forgiveness

Seeing the person as a person in need

Experiencing haunting nightmares of what happened

Overcoming hatred for the person

Other:

Exercise 8 Questions

Incident: 3

1. Have you expressed the hurt? Have you shared it with anyone?

2. Do you realize how it has affected you emotionally and mentally?

3. Do you still struggle with memories of the incident?

4. Which emotions come with the painful memories?

Anger

Hatred

Sadness

Depression

Fear

Sorrow

Other:

5. Do you realize who the enemy really is?

6. Have you taken the steps of forgiveness in the book? Why or why not?

7. What areas are you struggling with?

Speaking the words of forgiveness

Seeing the person as a person in need

Experiencing haunting nightmares of what happened

Overcoming hatred for the person

Other:

Exercise 8 Questions

Incident: 4

1. Have you expressed the hurt? Have you shared it with anyone?

2. Do you realize how it has affected you emotionally and mentally?

3. Do you still struggle with memories of the incident?

4. Which emotions come with the painful memories?

Anger

Hatred

Sadness

Depression

Fear

Sorrow

Other:

5. Do you realize who the enemy really is?

6. Have you taken the steps of forgiveness in the book? Why or why not?

7. What areas are you struggling with?

Speaking the words of forgiveness

Seeing the person as a person in need

Experiencing haunting nightmares of what happened

Overcoming hatred for the person

Other:

Exercise 8 Questions

Incident: 5

1. Have you expressed the hurt? Have you shared it with anyone?

2. Do you realize how it has affected you emotionally and mentally?

3. Do you still struggle with memories of the incident?

4. Which emotions come with the painful memories?

Anger

Hatred

Sadness

Depression

Fear

Sorrow

Other:

5. Do you realize who the enemy really is?

6. Have you taken the steps of forgiveness in the book? Why or why not?

7. What areas are you struggling with?

Speaking the words of forgiveness

Seeing the person as a person in need

Experiencing haunting nightmares of what happened

Overcoming hatred for the person

Other:

Exercise 8 Questions

Incident: 6

1. Have you expressed the hurt? Have you shared it with anyone?

2. Do you realize how it has affected you emotionally and mentally?

3. Do you still struggle with memories of the incident?

4. Which emotions come with the painful memories?

Anger

Hatred

Sadness

Depression

Fear

Sorrow

Other:

5. Do you realize who the enemy really is?

6. Have you taken the steps of forgiveness in the book? Why or why not?

7. What areas are you struggling with?

Speaking the words of forgiveness

Seeing the person as a person in need

Experiencing haunting nightmares of what happened

Overcoming hatred for the person

Other:

Exercise 8 Questions

Incident: 7

1. Have you expressed the hurt? Have you shared it with anyone?

2. Do you realize how it has affected you emotionally and mentally?

3. Do you still struggle with memories of the incident?

4. Which emotions come with the painful memories?
Anger

Hatred

Sadness

Depression

Fear

Sorrow

Other:

5. Do you realize who the enemy really is?

6. Have you taken the steps of forgiveness in the book? Why or why not?

7. What areas are you struggling with?
Speaking the words of forgiveness

Seeing the person as a person in need

Experiencing haunting nightmares of what happened

Overcoming hatred for the person

Other:

Exercise 8 Questions

Incident: 8

1. Have you expressed the hurt? Have you shared it with anyone?

2. Do you realize how it has affected you emotionally and mentally?

3. Do you still struggle with memories of the incident?

4. Which emotions come with the painful memories?
Anger

Hatred

Sadness

Depression

Fear

Sorrow

Other:

5. Do you realize who the enemy really is?

6. Have you taken the steps of forgiveness in the book? Why or why not?

7. What areas are you struggling with?
Speaking the words of forgiveness

Seeing the person as a person in need

Experiencing haunting nightmares of what happened

Overcoming hatred for the person

Other:

Exercise 8 Questions

Incident: 9

1. Have you expressed the hurt? Have you shared it with anyone?

2. Do you realize how it has affected you emotionally and mentally?

3. Do you still struggle with memories of the incident?

4. Which emotions come with the painful memories?
Anger

Hatred

Sadness

Depression

Fear

Sorrow

Other:

5. Do you realize who the enemy really is?

6. Have you taken the steps of forgiveness in the book? Why or why not?

7. What areas are you struggling with?
Speaking the words of forgiveness

Seeing the person as a person in need

Experiencing haunting nightmares of what happened

Overcoming hatred for the person

Other:

Exercise 8 Questions

Incident: 10

1. Have you expressed the hurt? Have you shared it with anyone?

2. Do you realize how it has affected you emotionally and mentally?

3. Do you still struggle with memories of the incident?

4. Which emotions come with the painful memories?
Anger

Hatred

Sadness

Depression

Fear

Sorrow

Other:

5. Do you realize who the enemy really is?

6. Have you taken the steps of forgiveness in the book? Why or why not?

7. What areas are you struggling with?
Speaking the words of forgiveness

Seeing the person as a person in need

Experiencing haunting nightmares of what happened

Overcoming hatred for the person

Other:

Exercise

9

Have You Forgiven Yourself?

Have you experienced any of the following:

- Tragedy resulting from a wrong decision?
- Accidental hurt or death of someone?
- Hurt of those you loved due to improper choices you made?

The book outlines the difficulty of what I call self-forgiveness. It is important to embrace and practice the principles of self-forgiveness found in the book.

Book Quotes:

"I had a very difficult time forgiving myself after my son's death. The tremendous guilt for not spending enough time with him and the shame for not being the father he deserved took their emotional toll. Days after his burial, thoughts of regret flooded my mind and depression gripped my soul."

Exercise 9 Instructions

If possible, read chapter eight in the book *The Next Level Forgiver* before doing this exercise.

For each incident you identified in exercise 1, answer the questions on the following pages.

Please be as open and honest as possible. It's okay to be unsure. The purpose of these questions is to stimulate thought and discussion that lead to answers and understanding.

To Dos:

Try to view your situation through the eyes of an outsider. In other words, write down reasons to forgive if this were happening with your friend or neighbor's family.

Exercise 9 Questions

Incident: 1

1. Write a few words or lines about the details of what happened.

2. Was this something that was accidental? You weren't aware of the outcome and never meant to hurt the person.

3. Did you do something to a person out of anger or frustration but never intended the results?

4. Were you dealing with an addiction that brought strain on your loved ones?

5. Did you make a decision, fully aware of the consequences at the time, but now regret that decision?

6. Have you asked God to forgive you?

Exercise 9 Questions

Incident: 2

1. Write a few words or lines about the details of what happened.

2. Was this something that was accidental? You weren't aware of the outcome and never meant to hurt the person.

3. Did you do something to a person out of anger or frustration but never intended the results?

4. Were you dealing with an addiction that brought strain on your loved ones?

5. Did you make a decision, fully aware of the consequences at the time, but now regret that decision?

6. Have you asked God to forgive you?

Exercise 9 Questions

Incident: 3

1. Write a few words or lines about the details of what happened.

2. Was this something that was accidental? You weren't aware of the outcome and never meant to hurt the person.

3. Did you do something to a person out of anger or frustration but never intended the results?

4. Were you dealing with an addiction that brought strain on your loved ones?

5. Did you make a decision, fully aware of the consequences at the time, but now regret that decision?

6. Have you asked God to forgive you?

Exercise 9 Questions

Incident: 4

1. Write a few words or lines about the details of what happened.

2. Was this something that was accidental? You weren't aware of the outcome and never meant to hurt the person.

3. Did you do something to a person out of anger or frustration but never intended the results?

4. Were you dealing with an addiction that brought strain on your loved ones?

5. Did you make a decision, fully aware of the consequences at the time, but now regret that decision?

6. Have you asked God to forgive you?

Exercise 9 Questions

Incident: 5

1. Write a few words or lines about the details of what happened.

2. Was this something that was accidental? You weren't aware of the outcome and never meant to hurt the person.

3. Did you do something to a person out of anger or frustration but never intended the results?

4. Were you dealing with an addiction that brought strain on your loved ones?

5. Did you make a decision, fully aware of the consequences at the time, but now regret that decision?

6. Have you asked God to forgive you?

Exercise 9 Questions

Incident: 6

1. Write a few words or lines about the details of what happened.

2. Was this something that was accidental? You weren't aware of the outcome and never meant to hurt the person.

3. Did you do something to a person out of anger or frustration but never intended the results?

4. Were you dealing with an addiction that brought strain on your loved ones?

5. Did you make a decision, fully aware of the consequences at the time, but now regret that decision?

6. Have you asked God to forgive you?

Exercise 9 Questions

Incident: 7

1. Write a few words or lines about the details of what happened.

2. Was this something that was accidental? You weren't aware of the outcome and never meant to hurt the person.

3. Did you do something to a person out of anger or frustration but never intended the results?

4. Were you dealing with an addiction that brought strain on your loved ones?

5. Did you make a decision, fully aware of the consequences at the time, but now regret that decision?

6. Have you asked God to forgive you?

THE NEXT LEVEL FORGIVER WORK BOOKLET

Exercise 9 Questions

Incident: 8

1. Write a few words or lines about the details of what happened.

2. Was this something that was accidental? You weren't aware of the outcome and never meant to hurt the person.

3. Did you do something to a person out of anger or frustration but never intended the results?

4. Were you dealing with an addiction that brought strain on your loved ones?

5. Did you make a decision, fully aware of the consequences at the time, but now regret that decision?

6. Have you asked God to forgive you?

Exercise 9 Questions

Incident: 9

1. Write a few words or lines about the details of what happened.

2. Was this something that was accidental? You weren't aware of the outcome and never meant to hurt the person.

3. Did you do something to a person out of anger or frustration but never intended the results?

4. Were you dealing with an addiction that brought strain on your loved ones?

5. Did you make a decision, fully aware of the consequences at the time, but now regret that decision?

6. Have you asked God to forgive you?

THE NEXT LEVEL FORGIVER WORK BOOKLET

Exercise 9 Questions

Incident: 10

1. Write a few words or lines about the details of what happened.

2. Was this something that was accidental? You weren't aware of the outcome and never meant to hurt the person.

3. Did you do something to a person out of anger or frustration but never intended the results?

4. Were you dealing with an addiction that brought strain on your loved ones?

5. Did you make a decision, fully aware of the consequences at the time, but now regret that decision?

6. Have you asked God to forgive you?

Exercise

10

Have You Recognized the Enemies of Forgiveness?

The book details several enemies of forgiveness, including ungodly pride, lack of spiritual maturity, and lack of expression.

If you can think of another obstacle to forgiving that has plagued you, please share it in writing or with the group if you're doing a group study.

Book Quotes:

In the Bible, the Apostle Paul shared the human dilemma with doing right. I will paraphrase his words found in Romans 7:21

Deep down inside, we all want to do the right thing, but instead, we end up doing the wrong thing.

Exercise 10 Instructions

If possible, read chapter nine in the book The Next Level Forgiver before doing this exercise.

For each incident you identified in exercise 1, answer the questions on the following pages.

Please be as open and honest as possible. It's okay to be unsure. The purpose of these questions is to stimulate thought and discussion that lead to answers and understanding.

To Dos:

Practice, in private, confessing the enemies of forgiveness that apply to you. You can do it in a room, your favorite place of prayer, or in front of a mirror. Use your imagination to do it in the most effective manner.

Exercise 10 Questions

Incident: 1

Enemy #1: Ungodly Pride

Do I display any of the signs?

Have I thoroughly examined my thoughts, words, and actions?

If this is an issue, how should I overcome it?

Enemy #2: Spiritual Immaturity

Do I display any of the signs?

Have I thoroughly examined my thoughts, words, and actions?

If this is an issue, how should I overcome it?

Enemy#3: Lack of Expression

Do I display any of the signs?

Have I thoroughly examined my thoughts, words, and actions?

If this is an issue, how should I overcome it?

Exercise 10 Questions

Incident: 2

Enemy #1: Ungodly Pride

Do I display any of the signs?

Have I thoroughly examined my thoughts, words, and actions?

If this is an issue, how should I overcome it?

Enemy #2: Spiritual Immaturity

Do I display any of the signs?

Have I thoroughly examined my thoughts, words, and actions?

If this is an issue, how should I overcome it?

Enemy #3: Lack of Expression

Do I display any of the signs?

Have I thoroughly examined my thoughts, words, and actions?

If this is an issue, how should I overcome it?

Exercise 10 Questions

Incident: 3

Enemy #1: Ungodly Pride

Do I display any of the signs?

Have I thoroughly examined my thoughts, words, and actions?

If this is an issue, how should I overcome it?

Enemy #2: Spiritual Immaturity

Do I display any of the signs?

Have I thoroughly examined my thoughts, words, and actions?

If this is an issue, how should I overcome it?

Enemy#3: Lack of Expression

Do I display any of the signs?

Have I thoroughly examined my thoughts, words, and actions?

If this is an issue, how should I overcome it?

Exercise 10 Questions

Incident: 4

Enemy #1: Ungodly Pride

Do I display any of the signs?

Have I thoroughly examined my thoughts, words, and actions?

If this is an issue, how should I overcome it?

Enemy #2: Spiritual Immaturity

Do I display any of the signs?

Have I thoroughly examined my thoughts, words, and actions?

If this is an issue, how should I overcome it?

Enemy#3: Lack of Expression

Do I display any of the signs?

Have I thoroughly examined my thoughts, words, and actions?

If this is an issue, how should I overcome it?

Exercise 10 Questions

Incident: 5

Enemy #1: Ungodly Pride

Do I display any of the signs?

Have I thoroughly examined my thoughts, words, and actions?

If this is an issue, how should I overcome it?

Enemy #2: Spiritual Immaturity

Do I display any of the signs?

Have I thoroughly examined my thoughts, words, and actions?

If this is an issue, how should I overcome it?

Enemy#3: Lack of Expression

Do I display any of the signs?

Have I thoroughly examined my thoughts, words, and actions?

If this is an issue, how should I overcome it?

Exercise 10 Questions

Incident: 6

Enemy #1: Ungodly Pride

Do I display any of the signs?

Have I thoroughly examined my thoughts, words, and actions?

If this is an issue, how should I overcome it?

Enemy #2: Spiritual Immaturity

Do I display any of the signs?

Have I thoroughly examined my thoughts, words, and actions?

If this is an issue, how should I overcome it?

Enemy#3: Lack of Expression

Do I display any of the signs?

Have I thoroughly examined my thoughts, words, and actions?

If this is an issue, how should I overcome it?

Exercise 10 Questions

Incident: 7

Enemy #1: Ungodly Pride

Do I display any of the signs?

Have I thoroughly examined my thoughts, words, and actions?

If this is an issue, how should I overcome it?

Enemy #2: Spiritual Immaturity

Do I display any of the signs?

Have I thoroughly examined my thoughts, words, and actions?

If this is an issue, how should I overcome it?

Enemy#3: Lack of Expression

Do I display any of the signs?

Have I thoroughly examined my thoughts, words, and actions?

If this is an issue, how should I overcome it?

Exercise 10 Questions

Incident: 8

Enemy #1: Ungodly Pride

Do I display any of the signs?

Have I thoroughly examined my thoughts, words, and actions?

If this is an issue, how should I overcome it?

Enemy #2: Spiritual Immaturity

Do I display any of the signs?

Have I thoroughly examined my thoughts, words, and actions?

If this is an issue, how should I overcome it?

Enemy#3: Lack of Expression

Do I display any of the signs?

Have I thoroughly examined my thoughts, words, and actions?

If this is an issue, how should I overcome it?

Exercise 10 Questions

Incident: 9

Enemy #1: Ungodly Pride

Do I display any of the signs?

Have I thoroughly examined my thoughts, words, and actions?

If this is an issue, how should I overcome it?

Enemy #2: Spiritual Immaturity

Do I display any of the signs?

Have I thoroughly examined my thoughts, words, and actions?

If this is an issue, how should I overcome it?

Enemy#3: Lack of Expression

Do I display any of the signs?

Have I thoroughly examined my thoughts, words, and actions?

If this is an issue, how should I overcome it?

Exercise 10 Questions

Incident: 10

Enemy #1: Ungodly Pride

Do I display any of the signs?

Have I thoroughly examined my thoughts, words, and actions?

If this is an issue, how should I overcome it?

Enemy #2: Spiritual Immaturity

Do I display any of the signs?

Have I thoroughly examined my thoughts, words, and actions?

If this is an issue, how should I overcome it?

Enemy #3: Lack of Expression

Do I display any of the signs?

Have I thoroughly examined my thoughts, words, and actions?

If this is an issue, how should I overcome it?

Exercise

11

Have You Walked through the Process?

I have shared much information in the book. Sometimes, it can be difficult to determine exactly where you need to start in this long process. I've summed up the process in three major steps.

1. Make a mental and verbal commitment to forgive.
2. Determine which level you're on and how to rise to the next level.
3. Understand which enemy of forgiveness applies to you and how to overcome it.

Please follow this exercise as it leads you through these steps.

Book Quotes:

"The healing begins with you. If you're not walking on the top level of forgiveness, you have work ahead. First make up your mind and commit to change. Do you see the value in forgiving and releasing the tremendous burden of hatred and anger?"

Exercise 11 Instructions

If possible, read chapter ten in the book *The Next Level Forgiver* before doing this exercise.

For each incident you identified in exercise 1, answer the questions on the following pages.

Please be as open and honest as possible. It's okay to be unsure. The purpose of these questions is to stimulate thought and discussion that lead to answers and understanding.

To Dos:

Share or write about which one of these major steps is the most difficult for you and why.

Exercise 11 Questions

Incident: 1

Step 1: I've made a mental and verbal commitment to forgive and change.

Things I have done:

Step 2: I realize which level I'm on and how I need to move to the next level.

Things I have done:

Step 3: I understand the enemies of forgiveness and am working to overcome them.

Things I have done:

Exercise 11 Questions

Incident: 2

Step 1: I've made a mental and verbal commitment to forgive and change.

Things I have done:

Step 2: I realize which level I'm on and how I need to move to the next level.

Things I have done:

Step 3: I understand the enemies of forgiveness and am working to overcome them.

Things I have done:

Exercise 11 Questions

Incident: 3

Step 1: I've made a mental and verbal commitment to forgive and change.

Things I have done:

Step 2: I realize which level I'm on and how I need to move to the next level.

Things I have done:

Step 3: I understand the enemies of forgiveness and am working to overcome them.

Things I have done:

Exercise 11 Questions

Incident: 4

Step 1: I've made a mental and verbal commitment to forgive and change.

Things I have done:

Step 2: I realize which level I'm on and how I need to move to the next level.

Things I have done:

Step 3: I understand the enemies of forgiveness and am working to overcome them.

Things I have done:

Exercise 11 Questions

Incident: 5

Step 1: I've made a mental and verbal commitment to forgive and change.

Things I have done:

Step 2: I realize which level I'm on and how I need to move to the next level.

Things I have done:

Step 3: I understand the enemies of forgiveness and am working to overcome them.

Things I have done:

Exercise 11 Questions

Incident: 6

Step 1: I've made a mental and verbal commitment to forgive and change.

Things I have done:

Step 2: I realize which level I'm on and how I need to move to the next level.

Things I have done:

Step 3: I understand the enemies of forgiveness and am working to overcome them.

Things I have done:

Exercise 11 Questions

Incident: 7

Step 1: I've made a mental and verbal commitment to forgive and change.

Things I have done:

Step 2: I realize which level I'm on and how I need to move to the next level.

Things I have done:

Step 3: I understand the enemies of forgiveness and am working to overcome them.

Things I have done:

Exercise 11 Questions

Incident: 8

Step 1: I've made a mental and verbal commitment to forgive and change.

Things I have done:

Step 2: I realize which level I'm on and how I need to move to the next level.

Things I have done:

Step 3: I understand the enemies of forgiveness and am working to overcome them.

Things I have done:

Exercise 11 Questions

Incident: 9

Step 1: I've made a mental and verbal commitment to forgive and change.

Things I have done:

Step 2: I realize which level I'm on and how I need to move to the next level.

Things I have done:

Step 3: I understand the enemies of forgiveness and am working to overcome them.

Things I have done:

Exercise 11 Questions

Incident: 10

Step 1: I've made a mental and verbal commitment to forgive and change.

Things I have done:

Step 2: I realize which level I'm on and how I need to move to the next level.

Things I have done:

Step 3: I understand the enemies of forgiveness and am working to overcome them.

Things I have done:

Exercise

12

Do You Realize It's Not About You?

In the book and this work booklet, I've spent much time talking about you, what you've experienced, the challenges you've faced, and the keys you will need to overcome. With so much discussion revolving around self, it is easy to reach the false conclusion that your life is all about you. But it isn't.

Yes, the pain happened to you. The hurt consumed your heart. The memories haunted you. The doubts came in a flood of emotions and left scars that seemed too deep to heal. But your life, including the difficult times, is not all about you.

You can use your scars as stars to encourage and influence others in need. Please follow this exercise to learn how to share your testimony.

Book Quotes:

"'But you don't know how it made me feel! You don't understand!'

Those are words people share with me when discussing forgiveness in private sessions. The people who use them aren't bad people or mediocre Christians. They are God-loving individuals who have been deeply wounded by something or someone.

In my roundabout way, I always attempt to help them come to an important realization:

> It's not about you.'"

Exercise 12 Instructions

If possible, read chapter eleven in the book *The Next Level Forgiver* before doing this exercise.

For each incident you identified in exercise 1, answer the questions on the following pages.

Please be as open and honest as possible. It's okay to be unsure. The purpose of these questions is to stimulate thought and discussion that lead to answers and understanding.

To Dos:

Write down some names of people you can witness to by sharing your testimony. When you find an opportunity, please do so.

Exercise 12 Questions

Incident: 1

1. What were the things that hurt most about this incident?

2. Do you believe others have, in some manner, experienced the things you did?

3. Despite the pain and challenge, is there anything you can thank God for during it all?

4. How can you use the hurt you endured to help others?

5. If others knew about the details of your struggle and how you've chosen to face it, what would be their opinion of you? Would they think you are a person of faith?

6. Are there things you regret about how you handled the situation? What would you change?

Exercise 12 Questions

Incident: 2

1. What were the things that hurt most about this incident?

2. Do you believe others have, in some manner, experienced the things you did?

3. Despite the pain and challenge, is there anything you can thank God for during it all?

4. How can you use the hurt you endured to help others?

5. If others knew about the details of your struggle and how you've chosen to face it, what would be their opinion of you? Would they think you are a person of faith?

6. Are there things you regret about how you handled the situation? What would you change?

Exercise 12 Questions

Incident: 3

1. What were the things that hurt most about this incident?

2. Do you believe others have, in some manner, experienced the things you did?

3. Despite the pain and challenge, is there anything you can thank God for during it all?

4. How can you use the hurt you endured to help others?

5. If others knew about the details of your struggle and how you've chosen to face it, what would be their opinion of you? Would they think you are a person of faith?

6. Are there things you regret about how you handled the situation? What would you change?

Exercise 12 Questions

Incident: 4

1. What were the things that hurt most about this incident?

2. Do you believe others have, in some manner, experienced the things you did?

3. Despite the pain and challenge, is there anything you can thank God for during it all?

4. How can you use the hurt you endured to help others?

5. If others knew about the details of your struggle and how you've chosen to face it, what would be their opinion of you? Would they think you are a person of faith?

6. Are there things you regret about how you handled the situation? What would you change?

Exercise 12 Questions

Incident: 5

1. What were the things that hurt most about this incident?

2. Do you believe others have, in some manner, experienced the things you did?

3. Despite the pain and challenge, is there anything you can thank God for during it all?

4. How can you use the hurt you endured to help others?

5. If others knew about the details of your struggle and how you've chosen to face it, what would be their opinion of you? Would they think you are a person of faith?

6. Are there things you regret about how you handled the situation? What would you change?

Exercise 12 Questions

Incident: 6

1. What were the things that hurt most about this incident?

2. Do you believe others have, in some manner, experienced the things you did?

3. Despite the pain and challenge, is there anything you can thank God for during it all?

4. How can you use the hurt you endured to help others?

5. If others knew about the details of your struggle and how you've chosen to face it, what would be their opinion of you? Would they think you are a person of faith?

6. Are there things you regret about how you handled the situation? What would you change?

Exercise 12 Questions

Incident: 7

1. What were the things that hurt most about this incident?

2. Do you believe others have, in some manner, experienced the things you did?

3. Despite the pain and challenge, is there anything you can thank God for during it all?

4. How can you use the hurt you endured to help others?

5. If others knew about the details of your struggle and how you've chosen to face it, what would be their opinion of you? Would they think you are a person of faith?

6. Are there things you regret about how you handled the situation? What would you change?

Exercise 12 Questions

Incident: 8

1. What were the things that hurt most about this incident?

2. Do you believe others have, in some manner, experienced the things you did?

3. Despite the pain and challenge, is there anything you can thank God for during it all?

4. How can you use the hurt you endured to help others?

5. If others knew about the details of your struggle and how you've chosen to face it, what would be their opinion of you? Would they think you are a person of faith?

6. Are there things you regret about how you handled the situation? What would you change?

Exercise 12 Questions

Incident: 9

1. What were the things that hurt most about this incident?

2. Do you believe others have, in some manner, experienced the things you did?

3. Despite the pain and challenge, is there anything you can thank God for during it all?

4. How can you use the hurt you endured to help others?

5. If others knew about the details of your struggle and how you've chosen to face it, what would be their opinion of you? Would they think you are a person of faith?

6. Are there things you regret about how you handled the situation? What would you change?

Exercise 12 Questions

Incident: 10

1. What were the things that hurt most about this incident?

2. Do you believe others have, in some manner, experienced the things you did?

3. Despite the pain and challenge, is there anything you can thank God for during it all?

4. How can you use the hurt you endured to help others?

5. If others knew about the details of your struggle and how you've chosen to face it, what would be their opinion of you? Would they think you are a person of faith?

6. Are there things you regret about how you handled the situation? What would you change?

End of Exercises

Forgiveness Journal

(This page has been left blank for your personal writings.)

FORGIVENESS JOURNAL

(This page has been left blank for your personal writings.)

FORGIVENESS JOURNAL

(This page has been left blank for your personal writings.)

Forgiveness Journal

(This page has been left blank for your personal writings.)

The Next Level Forgiver Work Booklet

Forgiveness Journal

(This page has been left blank for your personal writings.)

FORGIVENESS JOURNAL

(This page has been left blank for your personal writings.)

FORGIVENESS JOURNAL

(This page has been left blank for your personal writings.)

FORGIVENESS JOURNAL

(This page has been left blank for your personal writings.)

FORGIVENESS JOURNAL

(This page has been left blank for your personal writings.)

Forgiveness Journal

(This page has been left blank for your personal writings.)

END OF THE FORGIVENESS JOURNAL

(This page has been left blank for your personal writings.)

Other Books by C.L. Holley

Soar Above the Pain: Inspiration for Life's Difficulties

The God of My Midnights: Finding Him in Our Darkest Moments

Inspirations from the Scriptures: Daily Devotions

The Power of Christian Comfort

Angels Among Us: The Torrell Holley Story

Lord, Fix My Leaks: Unleashing the Woman of God in You

Visit http://www.CLHolley.org for more about the author and his ministry.

Made in the USA
Columbia, SC
09 December 2023